ABANDONED
EAST
MISSISSIPPI

DECAY AND DISCOVERY

JASON LYKINS

—
AMERICA
—
THROUGH
—
TIME

AMERICA THROUGH TIME®
An imprint of SUTTON PUBLISHING INC.
www.through-time.com

First published 2026
Copyright © Jason Lykins 2026

ISBN 978-1-63499-582-5

Typeset in Trade Gothic
Printed and bound in the United States of America

CONTENTS

Introduction:

The Call of the Hidden

I wasn't born on the Mississippi Coast, but since the late '80s, it's claimed me as one of its own. The Gulf's salty air, the hum of cicadas, and the sprawl of live oaks have become my home, sinking deep into my bones. But even as a kid, long before I called Mississippi mine, I was restless. The indoors felt like a cage—boring, predictable, suffocating. I needed to know what was out there, just beyond the edge of the everyday. What was hiding past the tree line, behind the weathered boards of a forgotten building, or in the shadows of places everyone else passed by?

That curiosity took root early. At four or five, I'd slip out of the house before dawn, while the world was still quiet and my parents were asleep. I'd wander the yard, poke through the woods, or stare at some crumbling shed, imagining what stories it held. Hours later I'd stroll back home, oblivious to the panic I'd caused, wondering why my parents were clutching their chests, eyes wide with worry. To me, it was just another morning chasing the unknown.

As I grew, my brothers and I turned that curiosity into adventure. We'd sneak into abandoned houses, not with cameras or notebooks—those were luxuries we couldn't afford, cameras might as well have cost a million bucks—but with nothing but our imaginations and a hunger to explore. We'd step over broken floorboards, peer into dusty corners, and wonder who'd lived there, what lives they'd left behind. Those places weren't just empty; they were alive with echoes, waiting for someone to listen.

Life got in the way, as it does. For years, the exploring stopped. Jobs, responsibilities, the grind of adulthood—they dulled the spark but never snuffed it out. About twenty years ago, something shifted. Circumstance, maybe, or that same stubborn itch to uncover what's hidden pulled me back. Mississippi, with its tangled, messy, beautiful history, became my focus. From the dark shadows of its past to the redemption in its stories of resilience, this state holds secrets worth finding. Some are heavy, some are hopeful, and some are still unfolding.

I'm an explorer, not just of places but of the stories they hold. Whether it's the rusted skeleton of an old factory or the overgrown ruins of a forgotten town, I believe history—good, bad, or complicated—deserves to be preserved. Through my lens and my words, I'm trying to do just that, one abandoned corner of Mississippi at a time. This time, it's the east side.

The Quiet East

East Mississippi feels like a secret whispered in the wind, tucked away in the shadow of its more storied neighbors. To the casual eye, it's quieter, less populated, less industrial than the west, where the mighty Mississippi River carves its legacy. The east side, particularly its southern reaches, seems to fade into a lush, green desolation. Is it the long shadow of Mobile, Alabama, pulling life and attention eastward? Or is it just the way the land holds its breath, keeping its stories close? I don't have the answer, but I've always been drawn to places that feel like they're hiding something.

Compared to the river-hugging west, with its bustling history of trade and turmoil, East Mississippi's past feels less sung, its tales less told. The landscape is dense with pine and oak, the air heavy with humidity, yet there's a stillness that suggests neglect—or perhaps preservation. It's not barren, not empty, but it's easy to drive through and think nothing much happened here. That's where I come in. As an explorer, I've learned that every place has a pulse, even the quiet ones. You just have to know where to look.

The east side's industrial scars are subtler than the hulking relics along the Mississippi, but they are there—rusted factories, overgrown rail yards, crumbling mills swallowed by kudzu. These are not the grand ruins of a booming past, but the quiet ghosts of smaller dreams, of communities that worked and lived and faded. To me, they are treasures, waiting to be uncovered. A boarded-up factory in Macon, a forgotten sawmill near Lucedale, or a derelict electronics factory in Decatur—they hold stories of labor, loss, and time's relentless march.

This book is about finding those hidden gems, dusting off their forgotten edges, and giving them a voice. East Mississippi may seem desolate, but its silence is deceptive. There's history here, layered in the decay, waiting for someone to step beyond the trees and listen.

1

BRICK HEART OF MACON

Sometimes, discovery comes by chance. Driving through Macon, Mississippi, my eyes caught on a striking brick building along Highway 14, its solid facade standing proud despite the years. I thought it was just another construction office, shuttered by hard times or bad luck. But as I stepped inside the old Boral Bricks Delta Division plant, I realized I'd stumbled into something far richer—a testament to industry and the human lives it shaped.

The place was a shrine to its own craft. Bricks were not just made here; they were celebrated. The reception desk, the columns, even a mural carved into the walls—all built from the very bricks this factory once churned out. Each corner showcased their texture, their strength, their possibility. But time crept in, as it always does. Water seeped through cracks, pooling on the floor, curling papers, and rusting metal. Scattered office supplies—pens, files, a forgotten stapler—lay like relics of a life interrupted. I wandered through the offices, imagining the people who once sat at these desks. Who were they? How did the plant's closure ripple through their lives, their families, their town?

The break room stopped me cold. There, in the dim light, a dishwasher stood with its door ajar, the top rack holding it open. Inside, coffee cups sat untouched, loaded for a wash that never came. It was the most human thing I'd found—a snapshot of a morning when work was just another day, until it wasn't. Those cups tied it all together, a reminder that these abandoned places aren't just buildings, they're where people lived, worked, dreamed, and left pieces of themselves behind.

The Boral Bricks plant wasn't just a factory; it was a piece of East Mississippi's pulse, now stilled. Standing there, surrounded by its decaying beauty, I felt the weight of its story. Not just of bricks, but of the hands that shaped them, the lives that depended on them, and the silence that followed when the world moved on.

Once the grand entrance; now a dumping ground for time's leftovers.

Above left: A tucked-away office nook frozen in silence.

Above right: A lone chair—just chillin', like it's on break.

Above left: Hallway to the break room, where laughter once echoed.

Above right: A dishwasher still loaded, waiting for a shift that never returned.

Above left: Cabinets crumbling like forgotten plans.

Above right: Code Red—emergency long past.

A brick mural faded but still standing proud.

Reception desk for guests that stopped arriving.

Above: Excellence award—no longer hanging, still hopeful.

Right: The main entrance atrium—once vibrant, now still.

A quiet corridor of empty offices.

Glass bricks filtering in yesterday's light.

2

UNCLAIMED STONES

Some places call to you long before you step foot on their grounds. Holcomb Monuments in Waynesboro was one of those for me. I'd driven past it on Mississippi Drive a few times, its unassuming facade blending into the landscape. From the road, it was hard to tell if it was still alive or already slipping into abandonment. Then one day, the grass stood knee-high, untamed, a quiet signal that time had taken over. Researching the place, I learned why it had fallen silent: Mr. Holcomb, the craftsman who had spent decades easing the grief of families with beautifully carved headstones, had passed away. His work had been a labor of love, turning stone into lasting tributes. I couldn't help but wonder what his own headstone would look like.

I approached with my camera, capturing the exterior and peering through dusty windows into a world frozen in time. Inside, I could make out tools, papers, and the faint outlines of a workshop where lives were once honored in granite. But it was what I found in the woods behind the building that stopped me in my tracks. Dozens of headstones lay scattered among the trees, unorganized, abandoned, as if I'd stumbled into a lost graveyard. Names, dates, and epitaphs stared up from the undergrowth, each one a story that never reached its resting place. The sight gave me goosebumps.

Were these stones left behind because of non-payment, families unable to settle their debts? Or were they discarded due to a craftsman's worst nightmare: a misspelled name, a wrong date, an error etched in stone with no white-out or eraser to fix it? I imagined the weight of that mistake, the costly, time-consuming process of starting over. Each headstone, so carefully carved, was meant to mark a life, to stand as a final gesture of love or memory. Instead, they lay there unclaimed, marking nothing but the passage of time.

Standing among them was eerie, like walking through a cemetery without graves. These stones were ghosts in their own right, tied to no one yet heavy with purpose unfulfilled. Holcomb Monuments, once a place of solace for the grieving, now held its own kind of loss—a legacy of craftsmanship left to the mercy of the woods. As I snapped photos, I felt the weight of Mr. Holcomb's work and the stories these stones might never tell. East Mississippi's history, it seems, is written not just in what endures, but in what's left behind.

Holcomb Monuments—carving memories in stone.

Above left: Headstones once proudly displayed.

Above right: A staged gravesite—part tribute, part illusion.

Monumental Office—where final arrangements were made.

Behind the scenes: the monument shop.

Headstones scattered like thoughts left unfinished.

Above left: Tossed without ceremony.

Above right: Like stumbling into a forgotten graveyard.

Sara Helen.

Above left: John Richard Harris.

Above right: Stone-carved reminders of lives once lived.

3

VANISHED OASIS

Highway 63 cuts through East Mississippi like a quiet vein, carrying travelers past places that blend into the blur of the journey. For years, I'd driven by a gas station along this stretch, never stopping. My tank was always full, my cup brimming, and the place seemed like just another pit stop in a sea of them. Then one day, it was closed, its windows dark, its purpose gone. Curiosity pulled me in, and what I found was more than just a shuttered convenience store; it was a snapshot of a life that once thrived.

The place had been picked over, shelves mostly bare, coolers silent without the hum of refrigeration. No cans of energy drinks or bags of chips lined the aisles, and the front counter, once crowded with impulse buys—cigarettes, lighters, cheap trinkets—stood empty, stripped of its urgency. But it was the discovery inside that caught me off guard: a Subway sandwich shop, not the sterile, urban kind, but one with a soul. A wooden country bar, lined with stools like something out of Peaches in Jackson, invited patrons to sit and stay awhile. Behind the counter, stainless-steel equipment gleamed faintly in the dim light, and a glass-doored cabinet for baking bread stood ready, as if waiting for the next loaf to rise.

I sat at the bar, closing my eyes, imagining the conversations that once filled this space. Farmers talking about the weather, truckers swapping stories of the road, families celebrating small triumphs—a kid's good grades, a new job, a wedding on the horizon. This was not just a place to grab a sandwich; it was a hub of country life, where the rhythm of East Mississippi played out over coffee and subs. The air still held the ghosts of those moments, even as dust settled over the counter.

When I passed through again recently, the gas station was gone. No bar, no coolers, no bread cabinet—just a patch of dirt where it all once stood. Another relic of East Mississippi, erased by time, leaving nothing but memory and a few photos to prove it ever existed. Places like this don't make history books, but they mark the lives of those who passed through. In their absence, I'm left wondering about the stories they held and why they could not hold on.

Fuel pumps gone dry—pumped out for good.

Saddle Up—last call was long ago.

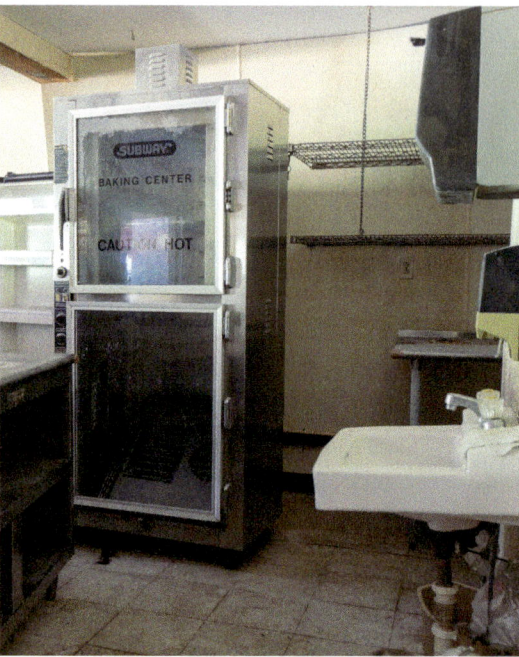

Above left: Did these ever even work?

Above right: "Fresh Bread" no longer promised—none inside.

Above left: Native to where? The past?

Above right: Try auditing this mess.

PETROSMART: not so smart anymore.

Empty coolers echoing with old hums.

Cooling days are over.

Above left: Shelves wiped clean of purpose.

Above right: "Winner!"

4

LAST WASH

J ust down the road from the vanished gas station on Highway 63, another relic clings to existence—a coin-laundry, as the locals call it. Not a laundromat, a term that feels too polished for this weathered place, but a coin-laundry, raw and rooted in the community it once served. Approaching the side entrance, I was struck by an odd defiance of physics: the door had disintegrated, reduced to dust and air, yet the knob mechanism remained, stubbornly clicked into the frame, as if refusing to admit the place was done.

Inside, the coin-laundry was a shell of its former self. A single washer stood alone, its companions long gone, while water hookups snaked through the walls, waiting for clothes that would never come. The cinder block wall, where dryers once rumbled, was punctured with holes—vents for heat and moisture that no longer flowed. Signs of a second life lingered: handbags hung from hooks, miscellaneous trinkets strewn about, remnants of a failed attempt to transform the space into a flea market. Someone had tried to breathe new purpose into this place, but the effort did not stick. At one end, the roof had collapsed, letting in rain and time, a reminder that this coin-laundry's days are numbered.

These places were once vital, hubs where people gathered to clean the clothes that carried the dirt of their lives—farm work, factory shifts, or just the mess of living. But as washers and dryers became cheaper, more accessible, coin-laundries like this one faded, their necessity dwindling year by year. Standing in the wreckage, I could almost hear the hum of machines, the chatter of neighbors, the rhythm of a routine now lost. This was not just a place to wash clothes; it was a piece of East Mississippi's social fabric, unraveling like the roof above.

Above left: Ever wonder why Coca-Cola still rules?

Above right: A lone washer stands its post.

Water flow interrupted—permanently.

Above left: A doorknob that refuses to quit.

Above right: Purses hang like a clue left behind.

Holes in the wall like cannon fire hit it.

5

Silent Chords

Tucked away in a rural corner of East Mississippi, where you'd least expect a giant of industry, I found the Peavey factory. Its doors stood wide open, beckoning me into a place that once hummed with the creation of guitars and amplifiers. Stepping inside, it felt like the last technician had just left, maybe fifteen minutes ago. The air was heavy with absence, yet traces of the factory's pulse lingered. Most of the equipment was gone, the assembly lines cleared out, but a few tech pieces—circuit boards, scattered tools—hinted at the work that once defined this space.

In the offices, I uncovered relics of a proud era: training manuals, tech books, and promotional materials, their edges curling with time. The lobby was a gallery of Peavey's legacy, lined with posters boasting the brand's name, celebrating guitars and amps that carried music from this quiet corner to stages worldwide. The warehouse floor, where instruments were once assembled, stretched out vast and empty, a hollow echo of its former life. I'm no musician, but standing there, I felt the weight of an iconic Mississippi brand gone silent, its closure a loss not just for workers but for the culture it shaped.

Driving by recently, I learned the building has been taken over by the local school district—a faint silver lining, a chance for new stories to fill its halls. But as I wandered through its empty spaces, camera in hand, I could not shake the sadness of what was lost. This factory wasn't just a place of work; it was a piece of East Mississippi's soul, where sound was crafted and dreams were strung into chords. Now, it's another relic, preserved only in memory and the photos I took.

Peavey! Once loud, now silent.

Golden glow at the main entrance.

The sound floor—dead quiet.

Vented subwoofers, once shaking walls.

A CD-R left behind—what secrets did it hold?

Application note—never applied.

Feel the power? Not anymore.

6

TIMELESS FLOW

In the rolling hills of Kemper County, just outside DeKalb, I found a place that feels like a step back in time: Sciple's Water Mill. Unlike the silent ruins I've explored, this mill still hums with life, its waterwheel turning as it has since 1790. I arrived on a quiet Sunday, the mill unattended, but the water still flowed over a small, wide waterfall, spilling into Running Tiger Creek with a gentle roar. The scene was serene, almost defiant, a testament to an old-era industry refusing to fade in a world racing toward modernity.

Outside the main door, a weathered box with a flip-up lid stood as a guardian of tradition. Inside, bags of stone-ground cornmeal and flour waited, offered on the honor system—a rarity that stirred something deep within me. I slipped some cash into the box and took a bag of cornmeal, feeling a quiet trust that's hard to find today. It was refreshing, a reminder that some corners of East Mississippi still hold fast to values long forgotten elsewhere.

I sat by the creek, watching the water cascade, its rhythm unchanged for over two centuries. My camera captured the mill's weathered clapboard exterior, the rusted roof, and the steady flow of the falls. I recorded a video, too, letting the sound of the water tell its own story. Sciple's Water Mill is not abandoned, but it carries the weight of time, its grinding stones—some 130 years old—still turning out grits and meal for those who seek them. It's a place caught between past and present, struggling to stay relevant yet proud in its persistence. As I left, with the bag of cornmeal in hand, I felt I'd taken a piece of East Mississippi's enduring spirit with me.

Sciple's Water Mill—grinding through time.

Water still flows, waiting on no one.

Machinery reduced to skeletal remains.

Leffel turbine—leveled by time.

"Honor System" sign still holding the line.

So many choices—and not expired!

Sign-in sheet still waiting on visitors.

Office entrance—silent but structured.

The mill pond's quiet back side.

Old equipment resting in earned retirement.

Years of history in this old mill.

It feels like it's asking you to linger.

7

ECHOES OF SCOOBA

A long a quiet stretch of highway in East Mississippi, the town of Scooba clings to existence, its name a playful quirk that belies a deeper sadness. What was once a living community has crumbled, leaving only a handful of buildings standing like sentinels of a forgotten past. The last structure on the row, a brick edifice that might have housed a store or office, recently gave way to time, its remains now being stacked on pallets, ready to be carted off for repurposing elsewhere. As I stood among the ruins, I imagined those bricks finding new homes—perhaps in a distant city, whispering Scooba's stories to anyone willing to listen.

The town's decay is stark, its streets quiet, its history fading with each collapsed wall. Yet Scooba isn't entirely lost to time. It is home to East Mississippi Community College, a place that gained fame through the documentary *Last Chance U*. The series spotlighted the college's victorious football team and the young men it served—players given a second chance to rebuild their lives after missteps. The college stands as a beacon of redemption, a counterpoint to the town's physical decline. Walking through Scooba, I felt the tension between what's been lost and what endures. The bricks may leave, carrying fragments of the past, but the community college holds fast, offering new stories of triumph amid the ruins.

With my camera, I captured the skeletal remains of Scooba's last buildings, their weathered facades and scattered debris a testament to time's relentless march. The pallets of bricks, neatly stacked, seemed both an end and a beginning—a town dismantled, yet poised to live on elsewhere. Scooba's story, like so many in East Mississippi, is one of decay and discovery, of loss tempered by the faint hope of renewal.

Old Row—ghosts of homes past.

Boarded-up storefront—closed but not forgotten.

Still offering trims—maybe.

The new peels back to reveal the old.

Feels like a Western film set.

Bricks salvaged for a second chance.

Remnants of a time we've almost lost.

DOLLY'S SALON

I n a town so close to being lost that its name feels like a whisper, I found Dolly's, a beauty salon that promised more than just a haircut. No, this wasn't Tennessee, and there was no sign of the legendary Dolly herself, but the name alone carried a spark of glamour long faded. Stepping inside, I was greeted by three hair dryers, their domed hoods like silent sentinels. Two stood tall, heads held high, as if still hoping for customers to return. The third had surrendered, its head drooped low, its spirit broken by years of neglect.

Against the wall, a stylist's table stood alone, its surface buried under a thick layer of dust, a testament to the hands that once worked there—curling, teasing, transforming. The air was heavy with the absence of chatter, laughter, and the hum of dryers that once filled this space with life. Dolly's was not just a salon; it was a stage for community, where stories were shared and appearances crafted with care. Now, it's a relic, frozen in time.

Outside, the town offered little more. Only the post office and an old building repurposed as a church showed signs of life, their persistence a faint pulse in a place otherwise crumbling. Around the corner, I spotted a facade being gutted, its bones exposed to the elements. Yet there, clinging to the front, was an old Philco sign, its faded letters holding out for another chance, a reminder of a time when radios and appliances were sold with pride. I snapped photos, capturing the dryers, the dust, the sign—each a piece of a town that refuses to be entirely forgotten. In East Mississippi, even the smallest places hold stories, waiting for someone to step inside and listen.

Dolly's Beauty Shop—
vintage soul, modern echo.

Salon turned gallery—
modern art meets faded
glam.

Essentials left like a shrine
to routine.

A heavy sadness lingers here.

The world moved on, but the signs never did.

9

Faded Pumps

In the tiny town of State Line, where East Mississippi brushes against Alabama, an old service station stands as a weathered monument to a bygone era. Its pumps are silent now, the garage doors rusted shut, but once, this place was alive with the hum of engines and the dreams of travelers. I could almost see it: cars pulling in for a fill-up, mechanics wiping grease from their hands, locals swapping stories under the shade of the canopy. Like so many service stations of its time, it was a heartbeat of the community, a place where journeys were fueled and breakdowns repaired.

Someone tried to give it new life, turning it into a store, but that dream faltered too. Inside, I found remnants of that failed attempt—empty shelves, a dusty counter, signs of a business that couldn't take root. The station's original purpose lingered in the cracked concrete and faded signage, whispering of a time when gas was king. As I wandered through, camera in hand, I wondered how many more of these garages will vanish as technology races forward. Electric cars are the new lightning rod, blamed for killing off gas-powered giants, just as gas cars once displaced the horse and buggy. I thought of the farrier, his trade erased without the outcry we hear today. Progress doesn't pause for nostalgia, and each generation finds new things to mourn, rarely glancing back at what came before.

Snapping photos of the station's peeling paint and abandoned pumps, I felt the weight of its story. State Line's service station is not just a relic; it's a marker of change, a reminder that what fuels us today may rust tomorrow. Its bricks and beams, like those of Scooba's fallen buildings, may yet find new purpose elsewhere, but for now, they stand as a quiet testament to East Mississippi's evolving landscape.

Again, pumped out.

Lee's Service Station—sign still proud.

Garage of yesteryear.

Service no longer offered.

Garage closed for good.

Another flea market, another memory.

Marlboro time: 1:05, forever.

The old store—now a shell of hustle.

Backside of the garage—where oil met stories.

10

HIDDEN GARAGE

I arrived at the Cumbest Saw Mill expecting the relics of industry—saws, motors, tables, lathes, the kind of equipment that once powered East Mississippi's timber trade. Instead, I found a treasure trove of a different kind: a collection of classic cars, parked as if time had stopped. A 1953 Oldsmobile 98 gleamed faintly under dust, its curves a nod to post-war optimism. Nearby sat a 1986 Lincoln Continental, a 1966 Pontiac GTO, a 1950s Oldsmobile Rocket 88, and, tucked in a corner, an old Yamaha motorcycle, its chrome dulled but defiant. The mill, it turned out, wasn't just a workplace; it had become a sanctuary for these automotive icons.

Speaking with the building's owner, I learned the story behind this unexpected find. His grandfather had stashed the cars here to protect them from Hurricane Katrina's wrath, hoping to preserve a piece of history from the storm's devastation. For a time, the mill's sturdy walls did their job. But on return visits, I noticed the roof had begun to give way, sagging under the weight of years and weather. Part of it has already collapsed, and I fear it won't be long before the whole structure caves in, taking these classics with it. Standing among them, camera in hand, I felt the fragility of this hidden garage—a place where one man's effort to save history now battles time's relentless decay. These cars, like East Mississippi itself, carry stories that deserve to be remembered before they're lost forever.

Sawmill turned quiet museum.

Rocket 88—like a legend frozen mid-launch.

Just like a jet, practically leaping off the hood.

Ready to roar, forever idle.

Lined up, awaiting a trip that won't come.

Red-light cone frozen in place.

Gran Turismo Omologato—fast days behind it.

Lincoln Town Car, luxury in decay.

A plush interior for no one.

Continental style, parked in time.

Decay down the aisle of what once was.

"You wreck'em"—says the ghosts of joyrides past.

Yamaha—speed and thrill long gone.

11

SILENT STORIES

In a forgotten corner of East Mississippi, I stumbled upon another graveyard of cars, an overgrown field where metal relics rest like tombstones. I expected to find cars, and I did—rows of them, rusted and reclaimed by weeds, each one a silent witness to a life left behind. Among them was a vehicle I'd never heard of: a Nash Ambassador, its once-proud lines now dulled by time. Alongside it sat familiar classics—a 1953 Cadillac Fleetwood, its iconic design caked in rust; DeSotos and Pontiacs, their chrome glinting faintly; Buicks sagging under years of neglect; and one that looked like a mobster's car, all sleek menace and faded glory.

The Nash Ambassador, I later learned, was a flagship of the Nash Motors Company, produced from the 1930s to the 1950s, known for its innovative design and comfort. Billed as "America's first family-sized economy car with a big-car feel," it boasted features like a unibody construction and reclining seats that could convert into a bed for cross-country trips. It was a car for dreamers, built to carry families across the open road, yet here it lay, abandoned in a field, its journey cut short.

Wandering through the overgrown grass, I felt a mix of nostalgia and dread. This wasn't just a junkyard; it was a graveyard, each car a marker of personal stories now lost. Where did they come from? What highways did they travel, carrying families on vacations, couples on first dates, or a lone driver chasing a dream? How did their paths converge in this quiet field, left to rust under East Mississippi's relentless sun? I snapped photos, capturing the Ambassador's weathered grille, the Cadillac's sagging frame, the mobster car's ominous curves. Each image felt like an attempt to preserve their stories before the field claims them entirely. Like the Cumbest Saw Mill's hidden classics, these cars are more than metal—they're fragments of lives, waiting for someone to wonder about their past.

The Nash Ambassador—dignity abandoned.

Cadillac Fleetwood still standing proud.

Mobster rides now museum relics.

Like someone just parked and walked away.

Dreaming of sunsets that taunt the soul.

All parked like a forgotten car show.

Look closely—someone's always watching.

The DeSoto, 1930s swagger intact.

1960 Buick Electra LeSabre, sleek and sleeping.

12

LIVES LOST

W hen I first rolled up to the weathered building, its stark facade and empty windows made me think it was an old hospital. But as I wandered its corridors, the truth became clear: this was a nursing home, a place where lives were lived out in their final chapters. A bright yellow sticker on a bed frame caught my eye: "Hospice." That single word hit like a wave, stirring a deep sadness. I stopped in that room, sat on the edge of a dusty mattress, and let my mind linger on the person who once lay here. They might not have been famous, wealthy, or a pillar of their community in the grand sense, but they were likely a mom or dad, someone who raised children to be a blessing, who loved and were loved in return.

I imagined their final days. Were they surrounded by family and friends, hands held, stories shared? Or did they face the end alone, with only the hum of the building for company? Fame doesn't require a spotlight beyond your hometown. Wealth isn't measured by a bank account but by the love you leave behind. A pillar can simply be someone who taught their children to respect their community, to contribute in their own quiet way. This room, this bed, held those stories, now fading with the peeling paint.

The nursing home had other secrets—operating or treatment rooms where lives were both saved and lost. One building, locked tight, kept me from exploring further, its sealed doors hiding potential sorrow I could only imagine. Another, closer to the road, had collapsed entirely, its roof and walls caved in, a deathtrap to any who dared enter. I snapped photos of the corridors, the hospice sticker, the rubble, each image a fragment of a place where life and death intertwined. As I left, my thoughts drifted to my own mortality. What will my final days look like? Who will be there, and what stories will I leave behind? In East Mississippi, even the quietest ruins ask the hardest questions.

Someone's final corridor, now cold.

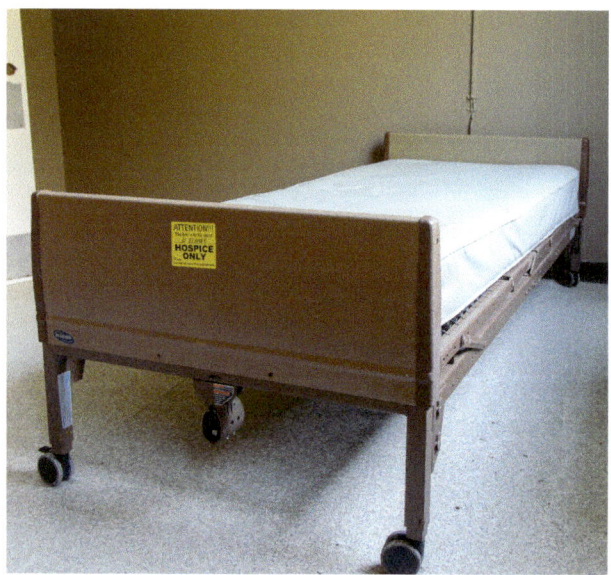

Above left: A bed without sound.

Above right: "Attention!" still posted, long ignored.

Bedpan cleaner—unused and still waiting.

Soap sits on the sill, untouched.

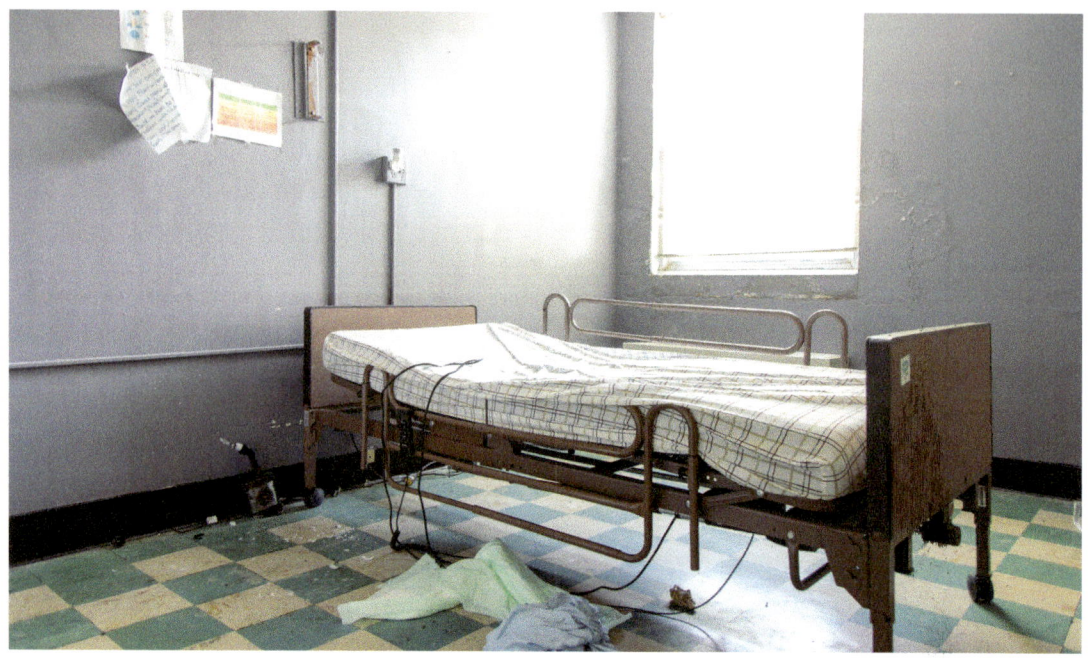

A note asking someone to please check in.

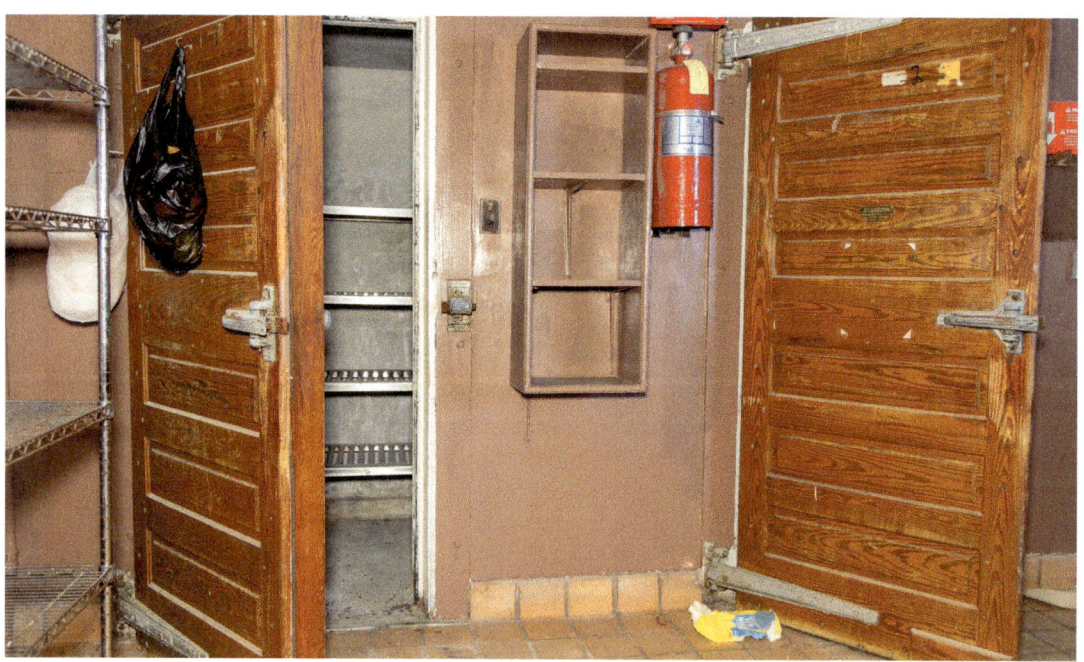

Wooden fridge doors tell the tale of age.

A doorway that offers a sliver of hope.

Above left: The operating room—hauntingly intact.

Above right: The X-ray viewer still lit with echoes.

Sterilizer—last used, who knows when?

The building on the right remains a mystery.

Locals call it "the death trap."

Report to the office—if you dare.

13

SILENCE OF REFORM

I n a place that feels like a sentence to solitude, the tiny town of Reform, Mississippi, clings
to the edge of existence. Once a modest stop along the old Gulf, Mobile and Ohio Railroad,
established in 1887, Reform briefly bustled with three general stores, a cotton gin, and a
sawmill, its post office opening a year later. But time has not been kind, and the town now feels
like it "almost was," its pulse faint, its buildings crumbling into memory. Among them, I found
a church, untouched since a chalkboard inside marked its last service in 1965.

Stepping inside, I was met by rows of movie-style chairs, their seats folded up, waiting for a
sermon that never came. Dust blanketed everything, a silent testament to sixty years of absence.
The windows, covered in tin, seemed sealed by someone who hoped the word of God might
one day echo here again. The simplicity of the building—unadorned, unpretentious—mirrored
Reform itself, a town that never grew into its ambitions. I stood among the chairs, imagining the
voices that once filled this space: hymns sung, prayers offered, lives shared. Were these seats
filled with families, farmers, or railroad workers, gathering to find meaning in a hardscrabble life?
Now, only silence remains, the kind that weighs heavy with stories left untold.

I snapped photos of the chalkboard, its faded date a marker of time's passage, and the
tin-covered windows, glinting faintly in the dim light. Reform's church, like the town itself, feels
trapped in a moment, waiting for a revival that may never come. In East Mississippi, these simple
relics hold the deepest truths, whispering of communities that tried to take root but were left
to fade.

Once a place of peace.

Simple design, timeless faith.

The church looks like it's dismantling itself.

The sign—illegible, eroded.

More seating inside than expected.

Pastor's corner, frozen in devotion.

Humble. Quiet. Devoted.

Leftover tithe records.

Thirty-eight years of Reform Church of Christ.

14

EMPTY HALLS

Reform, Mississippi, feels like a place where time has paused, its dreams of vitality fading into the quiet of a town that never fully took root. Established in 1887 along the Gulf, Mobile and Ohio Railroad, it once held promise with stores, a cotton gin, and a sawmill, but now it lingers as a shadow of what might have been. Beside the church, frozen since its last sermon in 1965, stands an abandoned school, its empty halls echoing the same stillness. Together, these relics weave a story of a community suspended in memory, their shared silence a testament to Reform's fading pulse.

The school's three entrances gape open, their doors gone—whether removed by the owner, the town, or scavengers reclaiming wood, I couldn't say. Inside, the rooms are mostly empty, stripped of life save for a scattering of chairs from the auditorium, left behind like forgotten props. But when I rounded a corner, I found the auditorium itself nearly intact. Rows of chairs stood in perfect alignment, still assembled for a lecture, play, or musical that never came. The sight was haunting, as if the room held its breath, waiting for students to return. Most of the windows, thankfully, remain unbroken, shielding the space from the elements a little longer, preserving the hope that it might endure.

Like the church next door, with its movie-style chairs and tin-covered windows, the school speaks of absence. The students who once filled these halls didn't leave by choice but by necessity, driven out by the lack of opportunity in a town that time forgot. I stood in the auditorium, imagining young voices reciting lines, singing songs, or listening to a teacher's lesson. Those lives have moved on, scattered like the dust that now coats the chairs. My camera captured the empty entrances, the auditorium's silent stage, the faint outlines of a place where futures were once shaped. Together, the church and school stand as Reform's last sentinels, holding stories of faith and learning, waiting for someone to listen before they crumble entirely.

The school, nearly invisible in the woods.

Surprisingly grand for its size.

Why the tagging? Why here?

A fireplace that warmed learning minds.

The backroom surrenders to time.

The auditorium—almost perfect.

Seats still face the silent stage.

She walks the aisle, imagining the past.

The front row has given up.

15

SALEM'S FADING HOPE

A little way down the road from Reform's silent church and school, I found another relic of East Mississippi's educational past: the Salem School in Noxubee County. Built in the early twentieth century for African American students and added to the National Register of Historic Places in 1989, this school was one of six consolidated from nineteen in the county, a hub of learning in a region shaped by agriculture and segregation. Now, it stands boarded up, its windows sealed against time, but a large sign out front declares an intention to restore it—a promise that stirred both hope and skepticism in me.

Walking the grounds, I felt the weight of the school's history, its classrooms once filled with the voices of students navigating a world of limited opportunity. The building's most striking feature stopped me in my tracks: a doorway to the second floor, inexplicably set halfway up the staircase. I'd never seen anything like it, a quirk of design that sparked my imagination. Who passed through that door? What stories did it lead to? The rooms were mostly empty, the hallway silent, but the structure held firm, as if waiting for its promised revival.

The sign's bold claim of restoration felt earnest, but experience has made me wary. Too often, such intentions burn bright at first, only to fade as time and dedication wane. I snapped photos of the boarded windows, the halfway door, and the sign, capturing a moment of possibility tempered by doubt. The Salem School, like Reform's church and school, is a testament to a community's aspirations, now left to the mercy of time. I sincerely hope the sign's promise holds true, that this place is saved before it joins the countless relics lost to East Mississippi's quiet decay.

The field's pride, standing alone.

From the back, like a New England postcard.

Patchwork bricks, scars of repairs.

The ceiling's burden finally showing.

Above left: A door halfway up the stairs?

Above right: Geometric wonder in an old school.

A window that's seen history unfold.

Above left: A newer addition, trying to blend in.

Above right: The story of the school preserved here.

The Historical Society breathing life back in.

From the air, Salem's still got it.

16

LOST EDUCATION

D eep in the heart of East Mississippi, where the world feels far away, I stumbled upon a secret that felt like a gift. While exploring an old store off a quiet road, my eye caught a glimpse of something through the trees—a cinder block facade, half-hidden by the forest. Curiosity led me into the woods, where an open door beckoned. Stepping inside, I found myself in a boy's restroom, the porcelain sinks and toilets miraculously intact. In my years of exploration, this was a rarity. Vandals, the scourge of abandoned places, often shatter such fixtures first, but here, time alone had left its mark.

I stepped into the hallway and turned right, entering what must have been the coach's office. It was untouched, a capsule of a life paused. A computer sat on the desk, as if waiting to share its secrets. Trophies gleamed faintly on shelves, their inscriptions boasting victories long past. Awards adorned the walls, each one a testament to achievements that once mattered deeply. Room after room revealed the same pristine state—desks, chalkboards, remnants of lessons left behind. I wondered if I was the first to walk these halls since the day the school closed, the silence so complete it felt almost holy.

Crossing into the gym, I stopped in awe. The court was ready, as if a flip of a switch could bring the lights up and start a game. The bleachers stood waiting for cheers, the floor unmarked by the chaos that often claims such places. I snapped photos, capturing the trophies, the gym, the untouched hallway, each image a vow to preserve this place in memory. As I left, I made a promise to myself: I would never reveal this school's location. It was too special, a hidden gem too pure for the world's careless hands. In East Mississippi, some secrets are worth keeping, their stories safe in the shadows of the trees.

Intact porcelain, oddly pristine.

Coach's office, frozen in the final whistle.

Vintage headphones for vintage learning.

Trophies still cheering in silence.

The library had its own private fort.

The school office paused mid-sentence.

The lunchroom—quiet but dignified.

The stage where drama lived.

The gym—modern flair meets fading echoes.

Ready for the final game.

The ceiling warns: the end is near.

Records that may never be heard.

Ghosts of library shelves.

17

HIDDEN PORTERVILLE

When I rolled into Porterville, Mississippi, I had modest expectations: snap a few photos of an old store, capture its weathered charm, and move on. But East Mississippi has a way of surprising you. As I approached the store, a young man greeted me, his eyes bright with pride and knowledge. He wasn't just familiar with the store, he knew the whole former town, its post office, mills, old school, and the descendants who still carry its stories. His words painted a picture of a place that once thrived, and I found myself eager to see it through his eyes.

Porterville, named for its first postmaster, Willie N. Porter, took root in 1887 along the Kansas City Southern Railway in Kemper County, southeast of DeKalb. By 1906, it boasted a population of 200, several stores, and a post office that opened in 1890. The Porterville General Store, now listed on the National Register of Historic Places, was a hub of commerce, while mills processed the region's timber and crops. An old school educated generations, its stone walls a testament to the community's aspirations. But like many small towns, Porterville's pulse slowed as industry and opportunity drifted away, leaving relics for explorers like me to find.

Guided by the young man's stories, I wandered to the old school, hidden behind a curtain of overgrowth. You'd never know it was there, its stone facade blending into the woods. Stepping inside, I felt the weight of time. The air was heavy with age, but a photograph on the wall stopped me: a class of students from 1939, their faces frozen in a moment of hope. It was beautiful, a glimpse into lives that shaped this place. I snapped photos, capturing the school's weathered interior and the picture that told its story.

My exploration led me to other remnants of Porterville's past. A dilapidated fire station caught my eye, an old ambulance parked outside, its faded paint whispering of emergencies long past. A newer fire station has taken its place further in town, leaving this one to decay. Nearby, an old house sat along the railroad tracks, its early 1900s style—simple yet ornate—evoking a time when trains brought life to Porterville. I photographed it, too, each image a piece of a larger tale. What began as a quick stop became a journey through a town's soul, thanks to a young man who knew its worth. In East Mississippi, you never know when a single visit will reveal a story waiting to be told.

Porterville General Store—small town soul.

VW Bug hiding in plain sight.

Store, bank, shop, and home—under one roof.

Where cars were once brought back to life.

Coca-Cola makes another appearance.

Two old sentries watch the world go by.

The gas pump—restored like a shrine.

Spring reclaims it—temporarily.

"Welcome To Our Porch"—still warm words.

Another woodland school, barely holding on.

Stones that whisper Old World stories.

What became of those who studied here?

A fireplace adapted for another era.

The stove's use long gone.

Retired chairs finally at rest.

Big windows once starved for light.

Bricks buried beneath fancy linoleum.

A lunchroom oven still waiting to serve.

Hiding its face from what once was.

Old firehouse, outshined by its replacement.

A home from the dawn of the 1900s.

Tracks that stretch into memory.

18

FORGOTTEN DREAMS

I n Meridian, Mississippi, where East Mississippi's quiet decay meets flickers of forgotten ambition, I made my final stop: Royal Land. Envisioned by A. Lloyd Royal in the late 1960s as a Disney-style amusement park, this was to be Mississippi's answer to a world of magic and wonder. Royal, a fairground owner, began collecting broken and abandoned rides left by struggling carnies at his adjacent fairgrounds on Sowashee Street. With his son Monte, he transformed these second-hand relics—a roller coaster, merry-go-round, Ferris wheel, and a train ride bought after a visit to Opry Land—into a non-traveling carnival. Powered by a half-broken generator and filled with refurbished relics, Royal Land opened with bright lights and carnival music, but its worn appearance and short lifespan of three to four years left it a fleeting dream, closed by the early 1970s.

I've visited Royal Land many times, drawn to the only remnant that endures: its entrance. Two concrete turrets stand proud, flanking the faded sign proclaiming "Royal Land," a gateway to a vision that never fully materialized. From there, a path winds into the woods, promising secrets hidden among the trees. Once, I ventured down it, camera in hand, but a kind lady emerged, gently asking me not to proceed as the land was private. I respected her request, noting the absence of "No Trespassing" signs. She acknowledged the oversight, and we fell into a warm conversation about the park's history, her connection to it, and its place in Meridian's memory. Since then, I've returned only to photograph the entrance, honoring the land's privacy.

Standing before those turrets, I imagined the 1970s excitement—children's laughter, the smell of carnival food, the hum of a train circling a quarter-mile track. Now, the path leads to little more than rusted tracks and a mildewed ticket booth, reclaimed by nature. My photos capture the turrets' weathered grandeur, a symbol of a dream that almost was Mississippi's Disney World. Royal Land's story, like those of Porterville's school or Reform's church, reminds me why I explore: to preserve the echoes of East Mississippi's past, even when all that remains is a sign and a memory. If you visit, be respectful—some dreams, though faded, still deserve their peace.

Royal Land's grand main entrance.

The main entrance within the trail.

The path that once led to dreams.

Bulbs that once lit up joy.

Amusement swallowed by time.

Blink and you'll miss this place.

CONCLUSION:

PRESERVING THE PAST, ONE STORY AT A TIME

When I set out to explore East Mississippi, I braced myself for a sparse landscape, expecting few locations and even less history to uncover. Boy, was I wrong. From the brick heart of Macon to the silent turrets of Royal Land, this region revealed itself as a treasure trove of forgotten stories, far richer than I ever imagined. I haven't included every place I visited—there are more historical gems hiding in the countryside than one could hope to capture in a single book. Each site, whether a crumbling school, a rusted factory, or a quiet church, holds a piece of East Mississippi's soul, waiting for someone to pause and listen.

My journey took me down winding roads, from the industrial relics of Boral Bricks and Peavey to the community hubs of gas stations and coin laundries along Highway 63. I wandered through fading towns like Scooba, Reform, and Porterville, where schools and churches stand as sentinels of dreams that never fully took root. I found unexpected wonders—a secret school untouched by time, a field of classic cars whispering of lost journeys, and the unfulfilled promise of Royal Land's Disney dream. Each discovery challenged my assumptions, revealing a region not defined by scarcity but by the depth of its past.

Why do so many of these places—mills, factories, schools—stand abandoned? Why do industrial sites seem to dominate the ruins, while homes and other structures vanish or transform? I've asked these questions often, and though answers remain elusive, the search itself has been my reward. East Mississippi's history, like its landscape, is layered with struggle, ambition, and resilience. Some places, like Sciple's Mill, still cling to life; others, like the Salem School, hold faint hope of restoration. But all of them, in their decay, demand to be remembered.

So, when you're passing through East Mississippi, whether along Highway 45, Highway 63, or any of the countless country roads that crisscross this land, keep your eyes open. You might stumble across history waiting to tell you its stories—a rusted sign, a hidden school, or a path that leads to a dream long gone. These places aren't just relics; they're invitations to connect with the past, to see the lives that shaped them, and to carry their echoes forward. Through my camera and these pages, I've tried to preserve a piece of East Mississippi's heart. Now, it's your turn to explore, to discover, and to keep the stories alive.